RHYTHMS

OF

THE

HEART

© Vkings (Kingsly Vunain)

Contact Info:

Emails: kvunain@gmail.com

21811879@student.ciu.edu.tr

FaceBook: Kingsly Vunain

LinkedIn: www.linkedin.com/in/kingsly-vunain-223406116

Address: Famagusta, North Cyprus,

zip code: 99450

Cover design: Ndzeh Cyril

Prove read & editing: Vkings

Rights to included pictures: rightfully reserved to their respective sources.

Brand Type: vkingsrhythmsoftheheart21

Binding type: Paperback

ISBN: 9798416787295

DEDICATION

To my lovely Mother

TABLE OF CONTENT

Ills & Societal Poems

Mother Earth & Nature Poems

PREFACE

Passion is like burning fire that never goes out. It has driven men from valleys to mountain crests; it is the crazy storm that drives empty plastics from earth far into the blue sky. It is the driving force behind the birth of this first piece of arts.

It all begins from within, the heart, everything we do: fear, love, war, people, and even the fine nature. 'Rhythms of the Heart' is a paramount first piece of Vkings poetry collection from over a decade, since 2011, while in high school. The author's passion for poetry genre of writing emanated from his love for short stories and drama. Inspired by O Henry in his 100 short stories collection, the author's need to manage time during busy schedules, his love for English expressions encoded in various genres of writings, his love for silent places, acts of loneliness, little verbal communication; the author discovered poetry as the best way to record his memories and experiences as a special kind of diary.

As time moves on over the decade, 2011 − 2021, the zeal to express rises above self into nature and society. In this respect, 'Rhythms of the Heart' is a selfless piece of 100 collected poems by Vkings; pregnant with not just self, but love and compassion, ills and society, love and intimacy, mother earth and nature, mother and family, war and sacrifice, hope and despair, African poetry and covid19 poems. The work is spiced with variety; with objective to heal or to kill respectively love and ills in society.

Simple enough to understand, the poetical diction or language/choice of words that flow through the poems are carefully selected, easily identifiable to readers with English as second language and of all works of life. The work captures the mind, the environment and things beyond. It is full of emotions: excitement, empathy, encouragement; all matters of the heart. The poems are mostly short, filled with rhymes and rhythms that sing a song in to the heart; and figurative language very common to the mind.

Spiced and interspersed with a high number of thought-provoking pictures, the book in each piece of poem paints a clearer image in the minds of its readers.

Each person, no matter their profession, age or gender, is sure enough to find themselves while reading through. The work captures: the young, the youth, and the old; medical, psychology, and about almost every kind of activity/situation the reader may be into. The book is an adventure full of surprises that none can afford to miss.

INTRO POEMS

This introductory section encompasses a mix of poems from all categories. It expresses the poet's passion for poetry and diversity. The section is loaded with a collection of ten selected poems from across all sections in the book. It prepares the reader's mind on the type of content they're about to uncover.

THE POEM THE POET AND ME

Sometimes I am the poem
Sometimes I'm just the poet
Sometimes they both I am;
Sometimes it's just a point
That makes my pen to bleed;
Transporting the way I feel
In a flow of mind to pen;
Squeezing out societal ills
To right the wrongs that kill;
Blank sheets they know my name
Emotions playing the game
As I wrap my words in tranquility
To shout out my silent noise;
Inspiration streaming from nowhere
Just as if I was there...
Overflowing my thought-full bounds
Out to the shores of society;
I know my words can heal
Broken hearts that no more feel;
I know my words can kill

Lifeless deeds society builds;
And if I fail to pen...,
I am a flood of pending emotions
Groaning in me like waves at sea;
I may not right to please
Or render peace at ease;
I write to light the right...
I come in all in peace
To render goodness at ease;
I am the poet the poem has poised.

Figure 1: **THE POEM THE POET AND ME**

WILL YOU BE THERE?

When the mornings come
And all the stars are gone,
Will you be there by my side
To wake and kiss me good morning?

When the sun is gone
And twilight is come,
Will you still be there by my side;
To share the shelter of my bed?

When my laughter fades
Through the anger of hard times,
Will you be there with your smile
To hold me and say all will be alright?

When my hand shivers
And my bright sight dims
To pen poems and passions of us two,
Will you be there to help me see?

When my bones grow weary
And my smile fading away;
As my face wrinkle about,
Will you be there by the chimney fire
To hold my hand and feel its old warmth?

When Heaven is opened
And my soul becomes foreign
Quitting this bodily vessel you see;
Will you still be there to cry me bye?

If it still will be you in the end
Even without this charm I see
But with this same heart I seek,
Then I love you without restrain.

Figure 2: **WILL YOU BE THERE?**

HERO

Every being is a hero
Born of human from zero
Whether in private or in public
All are able to make a topic.

Born of will and conviction
Fighting odds and conditions
Stranded enemies in confusion
And nature's laws in cooperation.

Born in chains like Mandela
Black or white like Obama
Freeing the world from rude killers
Just like the time of Adolf Hitler.

Born with a dream of tomorrow
Growing feet and thoughts to follow
Like a hunter's arrow in the forest
Making the world a better place for the rest.

BROKEN HOME

He thought of quitting
As little as he was...
Everyday getting worst
Hammered noise from the room
Life was better in the womb:
Where silence was a voice
Where love made no noise ...

He wished they grew old then
If old age could humble men
But they were young and stupid;
He couldn't wait to be alone,
To be a man away from home.

Day and night, hammers of noise
Drowning him in his flood of tears:
Mummy was beaten,
Who cared if he had eaten?
He cried without season
Everyday imprisoned
By pain without reason;
And when his tears had drizzled
In a lucky nap not a sleep,
He was awoken by another red whistle.

The feeling was killing,
His dreams were quitting,
The streets inviting,
As he grew in tears bleeding,
Where was he heading?

Figure 3: **BROKEN HOME**

PEOPLE DO

Love never lies
People do;
Love never dies
People do;
Love never fails
People do;
Love doesn't hurt
People do;
Love doesn't quite
People do;
Love reigns in all

But we're fooled;
Love is the key
Don't be rude;
Love comes to right
Tell the truth;
Love them all
Hate isn't good.

THE TREES CRY (1)
(In solidarity with climate change)

Men don't care!
All they want is their share
Of smiles and happy life;
But the trees cry:
Sharp blades that know no life
Murder their happy smiles
See as they bleed like the Nile
Cut from their umbilical ties;
Birds that flee and fly
Stranded in the carbon sky
Four legged in need of heights
They find no home to hide...

And when the angry sea rise,
Greenland a desert site...
Who else will pay the price?
Apart from you and I:
Barren soils aside,

Ozone layer funeral rites,
As the smiling sun so bites
Like hell fire when life dies
Where else will we now hide
When earth has lost its pride?

The future is you and I
Forget the dreams that cry;
Nature we kill without crime
To her we must be kind
Else we extinct our kind;
The trees cry...

Figure 4: **THE TREES CRY**

WITHOUT YOU

Nobody wants to be alone;
Needing you to call my own,
The greatest regret is me without you
Look into my eyes and see it's true.

Without you, I'm my own best company
Be my Chloe and I your Anthony
Looking into your eyes all day and night;
Like the sun and moon right from the sky.

Without you I cannot be me;
Offset by your absence from the scene,
We can make the greatest love story
Than Shakespeare's pen ever told in history,
I want to love you like nobody has done;
Even when this beauty I see is gone.

Figure 5: **WITHOUT YOU**

I WANT TO KNOW

There's someone in you I want to know
Someone with a smile of shinny gold;
The woman in you that makes me flow,
She speaks with charm in a voice so low.

I want to know you not just for a mo;
Forever I'll be your darling Jo!
Waking by you each day at crow;
And granting your wish without a 'no'.

My heart is young and wish to grow
The day is young about to glow;
No gold will shine for me to go;
Hold my hand into the love show.

Figure 6: **I WANT TO KNOW**

TO GROW OLD

To be old
Is to grow whole;
Escaping the snares of prematurity,
But old age is not for a majority.

To be old
Is to live with keen
Reducing the things that cause man to sin;
But is old age a fulfillment of dreams?

To be old
Is to retire from stress;
Disclaiming the youthful unrest,
But old age is closest to death's bed.

To be old
Is a sign of fulfillment;
Coming true to the biblical verse 'obey'
But why do the evil still grow old?

To be old
Is next to wisdom;
Correcting the steps of experience
But old age decapacitates the brain.

For the old, the young and the unborn:
The cry of a baby from womb escape
The dream of a youth in time and space
And old age will come to humble existence

Yet is old age hereditary?

Figure 7: **TO GROW OLD**

TONES and I

Stranger to my mind,
The presence of calm like the silent night
And together: Tones and I
Penning our honest thoughts for life.

So, this is my one dream,
That when I am gone in the Spring;
In the mist of the beauty of rising plants,
As per my Creator's utmost plan,
My tones will be there for life,
Penned in books and beautiful lines.

Smiling in my eternal sleep,
When I know the green generations fully reads
My own tones from days of old...
Then will I forsake the earth's hurt and go,
And Tones will dwell on for posterity's sake.

Figure 8: **TONES & I**

LOVE AND COMPASSION

This section is composed of poems with love that possess hurt; the tears and fears in love. It appreciates the beauty of love, with a focus on where it pains. In all, love is not a bed of roses; people fight to get their heart desires, and in all they either get rejection or acceptance.

TO LET HER GO

On the banks of singlehood
I found a lady ready to hook;
A fleet of suitors in her thinking room
Whom will she choose to make a groom?

She found the other with love and gold
But there was another she couldn't let go;
She met true love, but couldn't know
For all she wanted was one with the whole.

Perplexed in the heart,
Her choice will make some sad;
Leaving behind a river of tears
To hook the one she deems more Dear,
Selecting her pleasure from men pressure.

Choiceless men at the helm of her beauty
Will she choose whom is here and ready,
Or choose the one she loves so crazy?

I know not well myself...

And in their hearts; thoughts in battle;
"If I so go back to searching,
Will I find a sweeter beauty?"
But love is a president without a vice
Elected by a heart from a majority.

Figure 9: **TO LET HER GO**

THE STRANGER I MET

One night in a garden
By the solid shores of winter fall
As the wind played with happy trees
And their shadows danced in the joyful light,
While my body foamed with looms of cold;

Then came this beauty I've never seen
Her eyes were brighter than the beam light
Her beauty shone to scare the night
And all I could see was daylight in the dark.

She sat by, calm and cold
Flashing a second of a smile;
I couldn't believe the honor I beheld
To look upon her beauty from near
But she was so beautiful I couldn't dare.

So she sat by quiet like me
Enjoying that she came to seek
I had loaned her my cell to feed
Though she was unknown to me;
Rhetorical stimulus straying my mind.

We spoke in voice and silence
Unanswered questions within in violence
For our words were far less...
And all we said was speechless
Admiring her beauty with a heart so voiceless.

For every beginning, there be an end;

So soon time came for her to send
Her beauty back home from where she came:
Leaving her seat alone in the arms of cold;
Her smile still dangled on the spot
And her absence was all I could see...

As she left, I missed her baby breath
With me she left an endless perfume;
In these lines, I craft her absent presence
To keep her in a memory that never fades;
But O' what was that name she never gave?

Figure 10: **THE STRANGER I MET**

STILL THE ONE

She looked at the vacancy beside
Then thrusted her pillow aside;
Rolling over to the other side,
She wished her loved still reside...
It would appear he left no love
On the vacant space his presence fled;
All she felt was the cold emptiness
Sleeping beside without a choice;
Hoping to hear his usual voice,
She laid still without a word...
All she heard was silence speaking
All she saw was a wide ceiling
All she did was to blame her feelings;
Not letting go was a reason killing
Her love for him was still appealing
But she had nothing more to love
Aside the green memories in her mind;
And though his presence was absent
And gone like a shadow without a word,
He was still the one her heart imprisoned.

BROKEN HEARTS

Broken hearts
Are broken bottles
Fearless like wounded lions;
They bleed within saddened souls
Suffocating from the flee of love
Like fishes out of mellow waters.

Broken hearts
Are broken mirrors
Many pieces of a lonely image;
You wouldn't know whom they next will be
Fighting to glue their shattered bleed
Like mirrors never to be remolded.

Broken hearts
Are angry waves
Fleeing to the neighbor shores
To find refuge away from home;
And then they're back to the waiting sea
Armed like a soldier from retreat.

Broken hearts
Are dizzy souls
Longing for lonely grounds
To shade from storms of love;
Their wounds are deep than sea
Their pains they only can feel
Speech bound in their surge for words.

Betrayed on the wings of love,
They fall into the arms of depression;
Consumed by the friends of loneliness
And sealed in the cells of self-rejection;
Broken hearts are stronger hearts.

MY GREATEST MISTAKE

My greatest mistake was to know you
See all the clues you've let me through;
I had no foes, if not a few
You threw your ex for me like new
Now I'm loathed cos I love you...

See the prison you've sealed me in
There's no place I would rather be
Than here with you like twins in a womb
Watching over you like the nighttime moon
Would I say I'm in a living tomb?

See the mind you've seed in me
I never was jealous in my lonely glee
You came along with need to be
Now I'm alarmed by all those I see
Close by you like the shores of the sea;
Cos I know they might loot you from me.

Loving you was my biggest mistake;
Your beauty glitters by day like a seed
Men will go for nothing but gold

Am I strong enough to hold you whole?

I'm not saying that I loathe you...
You're the sweetest fruit Adam never knew
Loving you is my biggest mistake
Of which I'll always be proud...

Figure 11: **MY GREATEST MISTAKE**

I SEE YOU

I see you right through your eyes,
What's that pain behind your smile?
I know I'm not the perfect guy
But my love will stay and never lie.

I see you right to your heart
Spying the things that make you sad;
I know I can't undo your tearful past
But your smiles I will outlast.

I see you right through your soul
Is there a wound I do not know?
Dive in my arms let me heal you whole!
I'll shine like your sun till life grows old.

I see you in your every dark
I'm not bright like the sun at noon;
Yet even like the gloomy moon,
Let me light your every path.

The world is not my perfect home
I ain't one of them; hope you know;
In your heart I've found a lasting home
Let me be the guardian of its golden keys.

TO LET LOVE LEAD

Love is sweet
When we don't quit;
When problems weed
We judge so quick;
We sell the ring,
The love it brings,
And buy the wings.

Love will sing
For those who cling;
Like showers of spring
To spice life green...
Plant its seed,
Weed the weed,
To let love win.

Love will tweet
Its smiles on streets
When true hearts meet
And choose to cling;
To let love win.

Love don't cheat
Don't judge so quick;
Ego and greed
From hearts must flee
To let love win.

Love is king
That makes a Queen;

Problems inn
But melt unseen;
Love like sin
Stay like quit,
Give like greed
Love will win.

STRESS OF A LADY

It's stress enough to know a lady
They're all just like a baby;
Sometimes you'll think you're crazy;
Like wealth, she'll never come easy
Even though for you she's been waiting.

You'll talk love to her in a letter,
Keeping your patience like a waiter
"I'm sorry we can't be together."

Day and night fighting with her beauty
Yet when they come, she goes wavy;
What does she want! I think she's crazy.

She'll tell you true lies that are heavy
"I'm in love with another already"
Could this be true or she's just not ready?

You may steal her heart with just some words
Then she just realizes she's deeply in love;

But if you tease her bad, she hates like war.

Doing the things you normally shouldn't
To win her heart when you normally couldn't;
She will stress you like a math paper
Mining her heart for her chemical reaction
To catch the answer that feels her passion.

A lady is a study till life do part
Even when you've battled and won her heart;
Changing like a chameleon till you're tired
But for the sake of love, never retire.

Figure 12: **STRESS OF A LADY**

THE OTHER ME

I know sometimes I'm not the me you seek
But the other me doing things you do not wish;
I know sometimes the things I do you've never seen
Yet all along we've been together like king and queen;
Then I realize the me I know is not enough
Like a chameleon changing in all odds.

I know sometimes I go astray and my acts betray
Acting like a drunk to do the things that scare away,
Sometimes you've eared things you've never heard
It's the other me, the one I hide because he hurts.

The other me hides in me like a fish in the sea;
Sometimes jumping out like a dolphin to see
The things that go about around the mother sea

True sometimes I am full of surprises
It's the other me I know not when he rises;
And for the times we barked and fought,
I know the tears my acts may have cost;
Please forgive me; it wasn't me
It's the other me; the one that hides in me.

Figure 13: THE OTHER ME

Ex-OLOGY

You're a rare being in the human reign;
Needing the comfort of a man with brain,
Without your love, my joy is fake;
Leaving you before is my greatest regret.

I fell from the helm of your loving reality;
Scanning the world for another beauty,
Still I missed your care and charming concern;
Accept my prodigal love return.

I want to mend the heart my past had broken;
I'm sorry for the tears my flee awoken,
Glow into my eyes and see it's true;
There's no me without you.

Figure 14: EX-OLOGY

I'M SCARED

I'm scared of the things that make me smile;
They might leave me in awhile...
And if they're gone like the sun light,
My life might dwell like the night...

I'm scared of you when you say you love me;
Yet the feeling is such that I can't leave...
Imprisoned in your genuine love for me,
I'm yet scared someday you might leave.

I'm scared of the coming tomorrow
She might come like a piercing arrow;
Though I wait for tomorrow to make my dream,
I'm scared of the things she might bring.

All that is beautiful makes me fear;
The people, the things; gone, may bring me tears,
Yet I'm scared but I can't run;
I will be still till all is come and gone.

NO REPLY

I left you a last message without reply,
My heart gives me a thousand reasons to retry
Yet all I said was that 'I love you.'

I have been waiting on you like tomorrow;
Watching your moves all along in sorrow
Is it a crime for me to love you?

I still spy on you like the girl next door;
It's only you I still adore
But I don't know what to think anymore.

Sometimes I wish I could holdback my Words;
Sealing them all in my silent world
Yet I can't help because I love you.

Images of you hunting my mind
But I face this reality of no reply
Is this how we going to say goodbye?

LONELY

Love can be so honey
You both had a love story
Yet tomorrow you're lonely;
Was it because of money?

Life can be so funny
The love and care makes it sunny
And when we all hope for a life journey;
Tomorrow leaves us lonely.

Love today and gone tomorrow ...
It seems like love we borrowed!
Then we realize love has all been a shadow;
We fall in sorrow, but stand and follow;
Fall like leaves yet stand and follow.

But love is so funny...
When you realize you've been in love with you only
Sometimes we just got to be lonely.

Figure 15: **LONELY**

SHE NEVER WAS MINE

I didn't get a clue of her name
That was the greatest mistake I made;
I thought a second time was worth a wait;
But it all seems to be too late.

Days, I waited on the spot for so long
Hoping again her presence will fly along;
But all I'm left with all this while,
Is her fading perfume and smile.

My heart beats dance about
To the tune of the voice of her salute;
Her 'good morning' had a baby tone
But in a swift, she left me all alone..

Did they lie?
They told me love is patient
So I waited on a spot like a lame patient;
They told me to control my love desires
That I lust when I so admire;
See what the rules have done to my desire!
Confused of what love requires,
I think I need a love messiah.

I want to turn back the hands of time
To revisit that moment she passed me by;
But O' it seems just an illusion in my mind
Opportunity knocks but once in time!
How do I convince my heart she never was mine?

SILENT IN LOVE

Everyday I gaze and stare
At you because I care;
Wishing I could say 'I love you'
Yet afraid my words could hurt too,
Adoring as you stand and sit
Walking about like the beautiful sun to the east.

I love you solely in my heart
And when he comes to you so hard,
I am jealous like you were mine
So, I recount my heart solely in these lines;
Wishing you could see them
Even without my tongue...
And in lonely moments, it's you I long.

I remember the class and office desks,
And the smiles each time our eyes met;
Your beauty I gazed through the window,
Hiding and wishing it's you I have tomorrow;
But I'm a dreamer in the heart of silence,
Deep within, I know your stay will not be timeless.

TO MY TO BE

My heart longs for you, a dream to be;
Hovering, shivering and paddling about like a bee;
Like a plane, my love is beyond the clouds,
Hoping and wishing the future doesn't take me for a clown;
Until then, O' yes I hope your heart will give me a date;
Home alone and bed alone, where forth my soul mate?
Now unto the office of thy heart, I lay my quest;
Yet I dwell with an expectant soul; to thy heart a guess.
Should she be brown, black or white, let her be of kind heart;
Choleric or phlegmatic, maybe melancholic, yes to my ready heart;
Yet I now wonder; I'm I the perfect seeker to her heart?
For even in the Eden where we now dwell,
Many unto her the fruit of love; a dream for them too;
Yet, even in her jumbled heart, let her know I love...

Figure 16: **TO MY TO BE**

GOODBYE IS HARD TO SAY

You didn't love me
Did you?
I waited to say 'I do'
But all I heard was your silence
Then you stole away your presence
Like the sun at twilight.

Is it something I did
Or my heart just couldn't fit
Into yours to mold us forever;
Why can't we be together?

The stories are true
Aren't they?
You've found yourself another
Right in the absence of my presence;
You banged the door like the wind
Were you just a guest to my heart?

You fled and moved along
Starving me with your absence for so long
But my heart is still alone
And your absence is all I own...

Still wish I could call you Bae,
Without these gates I face,
I miss the rhythms of your heart
Each time I laid on your chest ;
I wish it still could be me
But to your heart I'm not even a guest;

How can we be on same earth
And live apart like strangers?

If I say 'goodbye'
My heart may rather die
Than hold that you're gone,
So I'm searching for hidden words
To console my lonely heart
Goodbye is hard to say.

Figure 17: **GOODBYE IS HARD TO SAY**

AFRICAN POEMS

This section is typical of African inspired poems. It expresses the beauty, natural environment and the pride of Africa. The section is more intimate to the poet; and in some instances digs out true and related life experiences of the poet.

MY AFRICAN CHILD

Today, I write for my African child
Looking deep into his sunny eyes,
So innocent and full of green life;
Sometimes it feels like he is shy
But he is the incarnate of love under the sky.

Born of a woman made of black,
He is the photosynthesis of true love in the dark;
And his coiled dark hair, his royal mark,
That huts him in creation's best art
And O! that voice with the sound of a lark.

I look again into those bright eyes
Seeing the future of a continent above its plights,
My African child, my song of life,
Proud to be, for he is his soul pride
And with the forest life, domestic and wild,
Born ready to change the world so wide.

Figure 18: **MY AFRICAN CHILD**

PRIDE OF AFRICA

Beautiful hearts of Africa;
Men and women made of black.

Born of cultures from long ago;
North, south, east and west.

We walk on ancestral treasures;
Cultures nurtured into our future.

Here we gather with the ancient drums;
Thousands of tongues united in black.

Sing and dance like the Egyptian maids;
Shout with spears like the warriors of Zulu;
Round and round the night blazing fire.

Strength of lions and tigers alike,
This is our home; our forest of life.

We craft the love and hunt the strength;
Caging our pride in our hearts; our home.

Born of the good roots into this hood;
The African hood; our aging pride.

This priceless shell; our culture;
In it we hide from foreign vultures;

Our boundless fight from extinction;
Our culture, our pride without assimilation.

VILLAGE ROMANCE

Do you remember the green village?
The songs of happy birds in the mornings!
Breezy green trees dancing with the wind!
Then the silent nights like the garden of Eden;
And nature's clock; the cock crow lyrics;
Day and night from season to season.

Do you remember the beautiful people?

Friendship jokes under moonlight's roof;
Grandpa's fairies from wisdom's room;
The spicy kitchen round grandma's fire;
And the foggy smoke raining teary eyes;
Then to the sky without chimney's guide.

So I wouldn't forget the village fancies;
Playing naked in the rains like babies;
Round and round every nook and crannies
Just like birds with no need to worries.

When life pins me down,
Dropping reasons for me to frown,
I'll spy back at the old time village town;
And wear a smile with a glittering crown.

Figure 19: VILLAGE ROMANCE

BLACK GIRL

Across earth for her replica
But not a clone even in Jupiter;
I found her in the heart of Africa
And yet by the shores of America.

I'm marveled by the tone of her smile
That lights like the moon in the dark
White molars on a backdrop black;
And by its shores, I found red lips
That even the roses can't beat
The cutest roses I've ever seen.

And how dare I so or ever forget
The swaggering flow of her walk
And the sensational click in her talk
Black like chocolate, sweet like coke
Beauty in strength like a black panther
O I found a golden heart for all people
Just behind the smile of her dimples;
And wow her deep dark black hair
Could there be better anywhere?
Such love and so much care
All want to hear and stare
Of the heart of a black girl.

I found true beauty in full
Product of nature school
Where is... her Sculptor?
Such a perfect Creator
Admiring His creation;
Marveled by her imperfection,
I'm yet searching for her replica
For her beauty is so uncommon
Just like the spark of a diamond.

Figure 20: BLACK GIRL

AFRICA ARISE

I heard the sound of a girl child crying
Wrapped in the arms of a man like a whore;
I watched a mother tomb her own child
Shot by a trigger from the hand of a force;
I saw the forest sinking like a ship
As it bled like the flow of the crying Nile;
Then I saw power doomed for life...!
Who and what is next on the news?

Stripped of the pride of our humanity
Everyday is force brutality
This is the venom of our reality
Are we humans or just a property?
Is supremacy the reality of this calamity?

In such a time as this;
While ego still fights with greed
Men ought to rise like seeds
To path a way for posterity's feet.

Land of glory; men paid with their lives
Beautiful mother Africa arise...!
If the powers that be can't unite us,
Let our color; less we be lost;
The wind mightn't catch the sun's rays
Yet it scares the clouds to shed her smile;
Africa arise like the wind of change!

My brother with the gun
Will you be happy if I'm gone?

Shot by an order from your heartless gun
Wouldn't you regret this thing you've done?

Entangled in the webs of fear,
What will we gain from our crying tears?
Should we dance in our fresh forests
Or cry in our rotten cities like pets?

If we scare from battle like babies
Our dreams will miscarriage as a fetus;
Africa without replica
One love, one word for Africa:
Arise!!!

Figure 21: **AFRICA ARISE**

HOME, SWEET HOME

Dreams draw me away from home
To beautiful places I have never known;
And I'll visit the Cypriot old cities
Remembering the legends and the critics;
But in me, home calls with charming pity.

Even when I cross the borders to beautiful France
Sailing by sea to the famous Caribbean towns;
And flying over the biblical city of Rome
Where I hope to meet the Spirit and the Pope;
With me, I'll still carry the flavor of home.

I cry, remembering the beautiful forests and plants
When I sight the cities here build up in the blank;
And for the birds that use to fly in the sky
Now city caged like criminals without crimes...
So, when I remember home, I cry...

No matter how long I stay in Rome,
I will soon lay my path for home;
Invited by my mother's kitchen spice I know
Home is not home without Mum,
No where like home, sweet home, here I come.

Figure 22:HOME, SWEET HOME

THE GOOD OLD DAYS

I may not have seen it all;
But I know of sometime ago
When love will never let go;
Though their pockets were goldless
And their shoes were toeless,
And sometimes life seemed hopeless,
Their lasting smiles went nowhere.

Whenever sorrow knocked at a door,
Solidarity will run from the neighbor's 'banda'
To 'sauver' a needy neighbor,
From famine and bleeding tears...

Oh, human love was such a pandemic.

'I love you' was a sweet story
Processed by ink and paper;
The single ladies happily jealous
When a suitor came to steal from their mist;
And daddy was never too busy...
His sweet love was proved by presence.

I remember the noisy streams
To which we ran from home
To play and swim like dolphins;
Cracking teeth as we shivered,
The swim was sweet and over.

So I wouldn't forget the neighbor's kitchen
To which we assembled like chickens;
Pulled by a breezy cooking flavor,
The food was sweet without error;
And soon we ran for the games we treasured.

Then came the Christmas saga
Where rice was gold to the tongue;
And all was new from head to toe
Even the pants no one could see;
All air gave way to kitchen flavors
Like an ambulance running in traffic;
Yet, all cocks and cows were so scared.

The cute old days
When the city was still green
And the trees didn't bleed;

To shed heads from the sun's heat
In trees the birds sang so free...
They're all gone like the Saharan wind.

Figure 23: **THE GOOD OLD DAYS**

MOTHER & FAMILY

Even if we're stolen by the world, nobody just comes from nowhere, but from family. Self is the most basic unit of society. Family collects a bond of love; not just by blood. Above it all, the place of a mother in everyone's life is paramount. This section makes a collection of family related poems.

MAMA

From the rising of my feet
To the rising of my soul,
Only love knows my place in your heart;
Your advice finds me when I'm lost
Your smiles light me when I'm sad;
I know your shoulders again on my pillow
Whenever I wipe my tears on it in silence.

I linger away, but never from you,
In my bed, I still feel your arms so warm,
In my sleep, I'm like a fetus in your womb
Dreaming of tomorrow as my day of birth;
Everyday, your loved baby without age.

I still feel your comfort when worries come
And your protection when the sun is gone,
Far from you, but never without you
Breath of your kitchen in all I dish.
Times I feel like crying so loud and clear
For your voice O Mama is still here to sing
My lullaby of comfort and happy peace...

I'm here alone, but still you in me.
Mama, O mother of my daring dreams
When storms arrive, it's me you choose
When the world rejects, I run to you
Without your love, every battle I lose
As you roar like a lioness at the friends of my tears
So I face tomorrow for you without fear...
Grown and earth beyond, forever your baby
Even when my heart is shared with a lady.

Figure 24: MAMA

MAMA DON'T CRY

Mama don't cry
Wipe your tears so dry
All is going to be fine
For I am here all the time;
When you miss me,
Come by my grave...
Sing that song you use to sing;
To lure me to my hungry dreams,
I miss you like dry soil misses the rains;
My time with you has been too soon,
Death came with a bullet to my heart
And with the flames from minds so dark,
All my dreams have sunk with me;
Even the home that sheltered our beds
My only crime was being a child;
Armless and defenseless day and night,
Don't cry for me;
For I wouldn't be there,
To wipe your tears away...
And feel your warm embrace;
Now I am back to the roots,
Wishing I could be born again
Please... Mama don't cry.

Figure 25: MAMA DON'T CRY

THE CRY OF A BABY

It cries, of which they should be sad
But if it doesn't cry, they'll rather feel bad;
It cries so sharp and lengthily loud
But all I see are smiles around.

Cute and fragile like a flower petal,
It's a bundle of joy from the world of the womb;
Up and down its little legs,
The best it knows is how to cry.

Minutes ago, a lady in labor
Crying aloud and begging for favor;

See as she now smiles like a new moon!
How come she forgave the pain so soon?
The cry of a baby is the quickest forgiveness;
It rights all wrongs from past without apology;
Even the kings arise from their thrones
To listen to its melodious tunes,
And dance to the beats of its music.

Cry so loud little baby
If this is what will make them happy;
Amazingly crazy...
A baby from a lady
Crying and stealing away pain and sorrow.

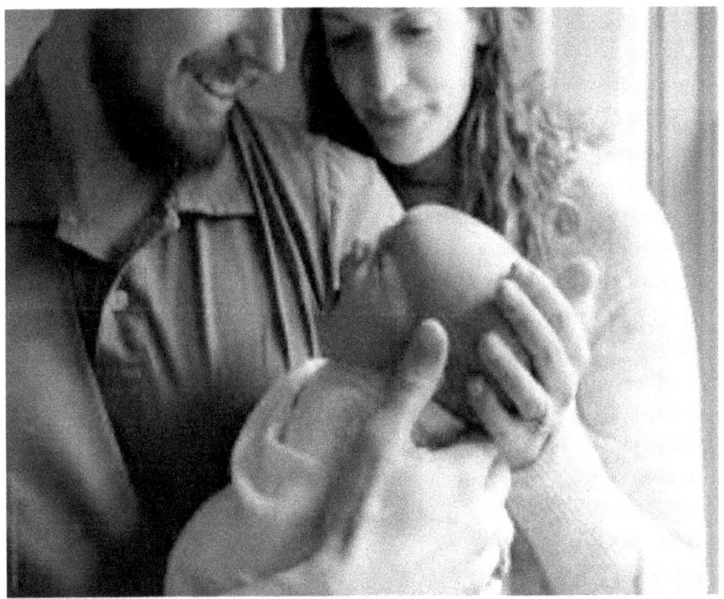

Figure 26: **THE CRY OF A BABY**

DIVORCE

Wife:
I married you for a good reason
But you took my smiles to prison;
Was loving you a kind of treason?

I swapped my dreams for you
To let you grow for us two;
But now I think I was such a fool.

Husband:
I ask not for you to leave;
Your heart was green like a leave;
Your ways as sweet as honey from a bee;
Back then when you were still my to be;
But you suddenly changed like a chameleon;
You were my dazzling one in a million...

The beauty I caught you with
You've buried in to this shabby dressing;
All you see is; as a man I must give;
Day and night, your nagging stink-sings like a bee;
Twilight in sight, home I long no more
Scared to open my battle-door.

Judge:
I do not support divorce,
But love is not by force;
For me my wife is a force;
Blind not the beauty for which you might not give up;
But now that your hearts are here in court...

Me:
Love can't count on the court alone
Let it still count on the love we own;
If truly we were found by love,
Then we do not need the law;
Love is free like the wind:
When she is soft, she brings the breeze
But when she is fierce she brakes even green trees;
But like the breeze at shore, love should always flow.

If together is a world of cat and rat,
Social distancing might bring you back;
Geographically quarantined apart for awhile;
If love found you, then love can heal you.

DAD's

We all have song a love song for Moms;
Forgetting to know from where it comes
We all did fill her womb for months;
Forgetting to know from where it comes...

Is Daddy a shadow?
Is he just a sofa in mommy's parlor?
See the scars in his hands;
Mommy smiles because he cares,
Feel the stress in his mind;
Carrying the burden of two at a time ,
And while his bones grow weary,
For us he toys and worry.
Dad is like:

The sky that carries the sun to shine;
The earth that shields mankind to live;
And the sea that makes the ship to float,
So we stand on the shoulders of a giant.

Mom is not an incubator; mom is love;
Dad is not just a depositor; dad is sacrifice ,
Without sacrifice, there will be no love
See how you glow like the sun at noon.

If I have to pen the space below,
I will fill it with a sea of words
To tell the unending story of Dad
Even when his strength has left the earth.

Figure 27: DAD's

MUMMY's DIARY

The cock was yet to crow
When her new day beheld,
The kitchen still asleep
When she plugged the lights;
She woke in the eyes of the night
Room to room with a smile
To watch her children sleep...
As she yawned like a Shasta daisy
At the wake of the sunlight.

Back to the kitchen prior to dawn
To make haste before night was gone;
And while the first cock crew,
Her chores were far from few;
While her world still slept,
She made their path a bed.

As the children left,
She rushed to make their bed;
A peep into her diary
The thought of it; so tiry:
Vacuum cleaner driving
Crawling baby crying
Market noise pricing
Kitchen fire frying
And while her hands were slicing
The clock was busy timing...

Then soon it was home
By the door full of hope

She stood with all her love
To welcome her whole world
Into the warm arms of her smile;
She took away their stress
With her bosom chest;
And when darkness awoke,
She sang them off to sleep
Tomorrow ready in mind;
Then she closed her diary...
What a weight she carries!

Figure 28: **MUMMY'S DIARY**

PRODIGAL FATHER
(Subtitle: Runaway Dad)

Every night by the shores of tomorrow
They sat like doves on the banks of sorrow
Waiting for a runaway father...
Like orphan and widow they waited in vain.

She heard your steps hurrying away
She drank Mum's tears back in the womb
Denied the chance to call you 'father'
Abdicated your throne before her birth
As you heard she was your fetus in the womb.

Born without a name to call 'Father'
She shared the lonely tears of her Mother
Envying the love of strange neighbors
As children played about their fathers
Was she just a mistake of pleasure?

She missed those gifts she's never got
She missed the embrace she's never had
She missed the lapse on which she never sat
And the kisses her forehead never found
She missed the voice that roars like a lion
To shield mother and her from the world
She missed the things only father can bring.

Now you're back like the morning sun
In search of her in her lonely sixteenths
What do you want; prodigal father?
To cajole her attention and steal affection

Or call you dad and spare the past!
And spare the rod and spoil you Dad?

You ran away and now you're back
To take a kingdom you never built;
With all the pain they both have gathered
And the traces of tears that paint their jaws
Like ancient ruins on a mountain side;
Are you that worth to be called 'father'?

Figure 29: PRODIGAL FATHER

COVID19 POEMS

Corona virus has been a hard pill for the people of planet Earth to chew. Many lives are those lost, many smiles are those gone, not by the gun but by an unseen enemy. This section, though with fewer poems, recounts the trauma the world has suffered from due to this virus.

HOMELESS

Devilish homeless virus!
To what do we owe this visit?
You play with lungs like toys,
Taking dreams to early graves;
And in our tears you find your joy,
Who the hell is your creator?

Visa free from nation to nation;
Traveling like a prostitute infection,
Even home is not safe with family;
Please take your leave so quickly.

A cry for the Doctors in battle;
At the war front without assurance;
And for your venom possessed victims,
Courage to the courage they carry...
A cry out to my own humble Creator;
Lion with eye-on from Zion and Judah...
The same One my Muslims call Allah;
Come down from heaven with power.

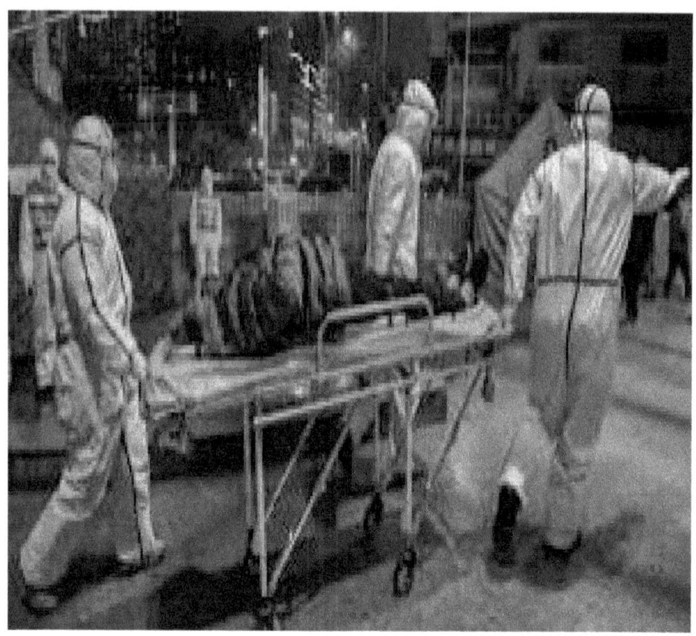

Figure 30: **HOMELESS**

PARADOX

I am a convict in my own home;
Freedom to the streets alone,
Masked like a thief in his wake to steal;
A rush from the invisible thief that kills.

Down the streets, a gaggle of pets;
Free like the wind from east to west,
Homely chores I must routine...
Tis the will of my quarantine.
Sunshine spy from window's eye;

Waiting for night to fall from sky,
Freedom's calling; but health is life;
Keeping my calm till the time is right.

Home alone in this bungalow;
Invoking Heaven to overthrow...
And when Noah's flood is done and gone,
Every tomorrow will be a brighter dawn.

Figure 31: *PARADOX*

LOVE AND INTIMACY

This section embodies a variety of poems that express the purity, desire and beauty of love. The poems are deep heart searching; and aimed at highlighting the true beauty love posses.

WEEDING NIGHT

There's a brighter future in the room;
Where is found the bright and groom;
On their first wedding night...

Blue candles from the dark room stand;
Soft music with a dance in hand,
And the gorgeous smiles so bright...

This is the dream of two lovers,
Locking the world outside the door;
And in, the two hearts beating in a magnet
To create their first fruit of matrimony;
It is the beginning of their love story...

THE PROMISE

In my dreams, it's you I still see;
On these shoulders it will still be me;
When tomorrow comes like waves at sea,
Even then, I long to be your queen...
With this toy we can make a ring...
To seal our love against the wind!

Our paths may part in adventure's dream;
Yet our hearts will stay with you and me.
For them you meet as you eagle the world,
Make the friends, but never share this love
For this is our love, our envious love...
It's you and me against the world;
Our promise of love as dreams come calling;
When childhood is gone and the future is come.

Figure 32: **THE PROMISE**

CRUSH on YOU

My love for you is still a desire
Baffling within as I admire;
What could loving you so require?
For I'll hire if I dare not acquire.

My unlaunched desires have all backfired
I'm burning within like a bushfire;
Times I've put on my love attire:
My courage, my poetry and my desire
But facing you will still backfire...

I admire with desire your beauty's attire
I've got the smile and swag you may require
More than your ex; the one whom you fired
But my intention is yet to be on trial...

I've tried to relocate my tactical desire
Drowning in guilt as my heart conspires
To call you a friend and closely admire
But even so, have still backfired
I love you but nothing to aspire;
For facing you is yet a desire...

Feeding my eyes with your beauty's attire
Even a goddess have got a desire...!
If just I could be your love satisfier!
Then I'll hunt the moon if that you require
But tongue-scared of your beauty's fire;
Could this be love or just a desire

To crush on you and soon retire?
Still I hide and crush till your presence retires.

FALLEN ANGEL

I saw you in my dreams when I was young;
Trying to paint an image of you back then,
All I had were pictures in my daring mind;
Patiently waiting for your presence to manifest.

I yet never thought earth could have such beauty;
So I imprisoned my dreams away from reality,
Certain that my damsel could only be a sky angel;
But here you're my dream damsel.

Now that I've found you like an earthly fact,
Waiting for you for two decades and a half;
I wouldn't stay away even for a night,
I still think you're my fallen angel from the sky.

Please tell me you so love me too;
For my heart has been an empty room,
Waiting and waiting for its coming moon;
Tell me it will be you on our honeymoon.

BEAUTIFUL IMPERFECTION
(subtitle: Woman)

A dazzling beauty,
She is romantic,
She is virtuous,
She is imperfect.

Her womb incubates posterity;
Her smile makes dark days bright;
Her presence spices discussion;
And O' that her charming voice;
It scares love from its hiding place.

The strength of a woman
Is the weakness of a man...

Woman is a spice of life...
Her presence is like the sunlight
Her absence is like the twilight
Without her, a house wouldn't be bright.

Sometimes she hates the things he does
Sometimes she nags and barks in anger
And though she might be void of power,
Her heart is stronger than a lioness's
She molds the home no man can build.

Treat her like a Queen
Then sit back and watch her win;
Though she might hate the things you do,

She will always be with you...
For when she loves; she loves so deep.

Figure 33: **BEAUTIFUL IMPERFECTION**

YOUR BEAUTY

Your beauty is enough to appease a God;
Framed on the wall of a diamond smile
Like the sun at the helm of the mighty sky
That melts the frowns of an angry soul.

Your beauty is deep right in your flaming eyes
Shining like the moon that lights the night
Walk with me through the dark streets of life
For your beauty is an undying light.

Your beauty is blameless at all curves

The handy work of a perfect Sculptor
Who else has seen such an original?
Just like raw gold from the heart of a mine.

Even the goddess of love can't still digest
The science behind your red rose lips
It's sweet like honey with a deserving kiss
Are you an angel dwelling with men?

And if you someday grow old,
It never will fade nor dare to go
For it's rooted in a heart with a pure soul
Like a river supply to the ever fresh sea.
You're beautiful, I wouldn't lie.

Figure 34: *YOUR BEAUTY*

COME MY BEAUTIFUL

Come my beautiful, come!
You've been away all day long
I miss the rhymes of your beating heart
Without your smile, day was dark
Come my beautiful, come!
Lonely's company now is gone.

Come my beautiful, come!
Spare me a kiss at your fore
Will you stay with me all through the night?
It's cold like sleeping ice outside
I crave for the warmth of your touch
Come my beautiful, come!

Come my beautiful, come!
Can I feel your breath closer?
Unlock the gates of your heart
And let me into its loving flow
Come my beautiful, come!

Come my beautiful, come!
Dance away your daylight stress
Soft music through the silent night
Close the door against the world;
Come my beautiful, come!
Me and you all through the night.

Come my beautiful, come!
Fear not, it's me your love
Come like a river flow

Come no more to go;
Now that the lights are gone
I crave the night be long;
Come my beautiful, come.

EMERGENCY ROOM

My love for you is critical
Your love for me is medical
Take me to your emergency room
I need the surgery to be your groom.

I am a victim of love's deception
Bleeding at your heart's reception
Evacuate me to an emergent location
I long for the romance of your operation.

I'm not in a rush like an ambulance,
But without your touch, I'll loose balance
Haste me to your emergency room
Anesthetic to my pain and wounds
I need the surgery to be your groom.

Figure 35: EMERGENCY ROOM

PANTING OVER YOU

I'm panting over you like a running deer
Losing your love is still my only fear;
Sometimes I think I'm running mad
Breaking the rules to catch your heart
And be your host to the end of time
But I'm still a stranger to your lonely heart.

I've found in you a golden song
That draws my soul to your warm embrace,
Like a worship song the Christians raise
To draw the Spirit with heavenly grace.

I'm running, none stop, like a river flow
Hoping your heart will beat more slow
For I'm not a pro but can make you glow;
If only I can win this race to know...

I know I'm not alone in this loving race;
Men of my kind scrambling for a place
In your lonely heart, where beauty reigns;
So I've come at the speed of sunlight
Braking the clouds all through the sky
To catch your love and call you mine.

But I'm still on the knowing you stress
Ascending your heart like Mount Everest.

Figure 36: **PANTING OVER YOU**

ALONG THE NILE

I've had this chance to know your smile
You're beautiful I wouldn't lie;
You and I across the Nile
To flirt the water with our eyes
Along together without a bye...

We'll sing our song in the noisy light
And fold ourselves across the night;
Floating thus far away from sight
To the place our gentle boat alight...

Needless to google a happier smile
When I'm here by your lonely side
To scare away your daring fright
As we float down the Nile of life.

Figure 37: ALONG THE NILE

LIFETIME COACH

My little life never genesisized with you
But I dream its revelation with you;
My heart is allergic to the echo of 'no'
So I waited for the lyrics of your 'yes'
For no reason will I let you go
Please be my forever guest
I want to treat you like each day is last
Forgive me if sometimes I make you sad.

Let me dance to every beat of your heart
Listening to its resounding echoes of love
You're my relevant type of lady
The rose who drives me crazy
With you I dream a baby

I didn't retire from the knowing you stress
For I knew with you, I'll be my best;
We may not drive round the city in a porch
But you should know; you're my lifetime coach.

WHEN I'M WITH YOU

When duty calls me from home,
Away I feel so alone;
Even when I call on the phone,
To hear the voice of my own,
I still feel so alone.

I sneak through traffic like water

To rush home to my love driver;
I horn the door with a smile
To fall in the arms of my only size.

With you I know of a goddess
That buys away all my sadness;
With you I'm free from lust
Lusting after the only one that cost;
Everyday I know of same kiss
From the only one my heart so please;
And while I watch as you sleep,
I still wish the morning doesn't peep
Cause duty will take me away from you with greed;
When I'm with you my world is so free.

Figure 38: **WHEN I'M WITH YOU**

MINGLE

Mingle if you're single
A touch of love can tingle,

Mingle and let hearts cringle
Wedding bells yearn to jingle,

Mingle till love grows wrinkles
Many are the dares to dribble,

Mingle, even single is not simple
But love is for two not triple,

Mingle for the smiles to sprinkle
Mingle; lost love can be rekindled,

Mingle or plough in the single
Single or mingle, not middle,

Singles, are you ready to mingle?
Mingle and never be single
True love is born for people,

Mingle now and never belittle
New days bring but wrinkles.

YOUR EYES

Your eyes are the prettiest daughters of the sun
Whenever I spy them; I wish you could be mine;
So I can wake by your side earlier each morning
And pause by the shoulders of our sleeping bed
To savor the rise of your diamond eyes like the sun.

Even mother sun peeps
Through the window each morning
To admire the rise of your pretty eyes
And then she goes in wonder to the sky
Thinking she met the brightest stars of the night
As she marvels in a soliloquy through the day.

And yes! They're the brightest stars in the sky
Even the moon is jealous at night
Whenever it meets the beam from your eyes
You're beauty; I wouldn't lie.

So I wonder in my desires
What falling in love with you will be like;
And in my wonder, I so admire:
Your lips, your smile, your eyes...
Those eyes that charm even the sun.

Yes it's your heart I seek
But in your eyes it's me I see;
If I could be your to be even for a day,
Even if loving you is a sin,
Then I vow I wouldn't repent
For your eyes are the mirror of my soul.

Figure 39: YOUR EYES

YOU LEFT

I thought you came to stay
But my heart you stole away;
Without you my heart is jobless
For loving you was it's lone profession;
I thought our love will never retire
But I'm back in the streets like a love seeker.

I remember the knowing you stress
Running like text to prove my best
To your heart I was still a guess...
And the messages that ran in morning cold
To deliver warmth in your early bed.

You left not even a 'bye'
Demolishing your heart without notice
And the smiles we shared, you took away
I'm back to the streets like a hocker
And the wages of my love are frozen
Like the bank account of a love hacker.

Behind you left a broken heart
Behind you left a hopeless soul
Behind you left a sunless smile
I'm still addicted to your presence.

If you were gone like the sun in the sky
Then I know I will see you again;
If you were gone like the moon in the night
Then I know I will see you again;
But you're gone like rain drops

Into the summer soils...
Lost from sight like the wind.

I miss the venom of your smiles
I miss the music of your baby voice;
And have you forgotten the sweet names:
Honey, love; the... of my dreams...?
In your absence, still I feel you're here.

And for this piece I write of you,
I'll paste along the world streets
To alert of my missing rib;
For there's no Adam without Eve...
Should you come across its lonely sheet,
Please find your way back to me...

Figure 40: YOU LEFT

DANCE WITH ME

Do you care for some music?
I've got the words to quake your feelings;
Tonight, let me be your song writer
Or at the min your dance guitar
To play for you some sweet melody;
To steal you from the cage of your stress
And shield you in the frames of my arms to rest.

Just you and I
With melody of birds in the chorus line
At the helm of the yawning twilight;
Dance like the trees in the arms of the wind,
Close your eyes and feel the swing
Loose you free, I won't let you fall
And if it please just fall in love;
Yet if to sleep, I'll be your guard.

Dance with me closer my lady;
Close your eyes and drive me crazy;
Into my arms like my fragile baby;
Forget the world that drives you crazy
Dance with me throughout the night
Dance with me to dawn rebirth;
Dance with me O' my lady.

Figure 41: **DANCE WITH ME**

YOUR LIPS

Your lips are the cutest roses I've ever seen
The sweetest place my lips have ever been
If there be a thing sweeter than honey,
It's the taste of your rosy-red lips;
The beautiful gates that fence your smile
And shield your immaculate white molars.

I long for another day our lips may meet
Whether in love, luck or infatuation
To form the eclipse of another kiss

Like the moon in the sky that kisses the sun;
And if some day you're gone like the sun,
I'll carry the taste of your honey lips
Like the moon into the darks of your absence;
Yet I'll miss the aroma of your breath
That I savor only when I'm on your lips.

Figure 42: **YOUR LIPS**

A HEART THAT LOVES

A heart that loves, so worried
A heart that loves, so sorry,
A heart that loves, so truthful
A heart that loves, so beautiful,
A heart that loves, so caring
A heart that loves, so daring,
A heart that loves, so mindful
A heart that loves, so grateful,
A heart that loves, so merciful
A heart that loves, so peaceful,
A heart that loves, so faithful
A heart that loves, so joyful,
A heart that loves, so fragile
A heart that loves, never dies.

AMANDA

Will you be my heart commander?
With you; no retreat, no surrender;
Take my heart to the love arena!
And if I fight like a love pretender,
Throw my love across the enemy border;
Amanda, my love-commander
I want to be your sole defender;
To pierce your fears like a deer hunter,
Loving you without surrender.

When the enemy will thunder
Raining your tears to the gutter;

I'll shield you like a soldier...
Amanda my love commander,
I love you like the 'Black Panther'
I love you without surrender.

YOUR SMILE

It's the quickest gift you've ever got
To give another without a cost;
It hides within a complex face
It comes and goes without a trace;
To lend a way for the face to frown
But the smile is the best of facial crowns.

It comes like the sun when clouds escape
To scare the frowns that come to dare;
It comes like the moon to glow the dark
And tell mankind in there is love.

Why fake your smile to scam some love?
You've got the frowns to share the hate!
Smiles are born with love like twins
Frowns are dug from hateful scenes;
To frown or smile is not a sin
But smile is a cure for every being.

When dark days come and seem to scare

You've got a smile to stand and dare
At war, in pain, a smile to share
To tell your fears you're stronger than hell.

It metamorphosis into laughter:
To gain a voice and make some noise,
And handicap the scares of a saddened face;
Forget the hurt, smile and drive...
Yet in every smile, spare your limits
Just like the bounds of falling rain.

Figure 43: YOUR SMILE

ILLS & SOCIETAL POEMS

This section is filled with a spice of critical societal poems of various categories. It deals more with addressing societal ills; with the objective to effect change in human societal interactions. It advocates for care, where there is none; and cries with those who cry. It is made up more of sad, empathetic and emotional poems.

FOR THE FORGOTTEN

My heart bleeds for society
As I walk across with anxiety
I see hungry stomachs in the street
I see passing men full of greed;
I see the sun on them as it heats
Little children without what to eat
The search for food is their only dream
O! My tears roll down like a stream,
All we want is our fare;
Do we care ever to share?

As I walk across the city cells,
I see Innocence locked in shells
Their crime is that they did nothing
Justice doesn't care to do something;
Their only dream is to leave prison
Why are they caged without reason?

I heard a cry from a mother's womb,
I saw the drugs force it to succumb
Denied the chance to live life like me;
What is the crime of a fetus being?

They're forgotten like fallen leaves of a tree
Denied the rights to live and be free;
I may not have the might to change like a God,
But this is my scream of attention call!

THE STREET BEETLE (1)
(In solidarity with street children)

I heard a sound from the streets
Perhaps it came from the trees
Clapping for the singing wind
And as I braced to the spying window,
O no! twas the cry of a child
No more eligible to smile:
Grabbed in the arms of angry winter
In the night when blankets are sweeter.

As I watched through the window,
I caught a childless widow
Sneak out of her resting home
With food that gave him hope;
She bereaved his eyes from tears
And stole away his fears;

And though it might have been little,
She saved the helpless beetle...
With that, she bought him a smile
Then came a silent night.

He was yet to graduate his smiles
When cold admitted new frowns
And within, he fought with the night
Hoping the merciful sun will soon smile;
To let him out like a soul freed from hell.

If all men do is pray,
Then they lead miracles astray;
Men are vessels mankind has got
To save kindness from sudden rust,
It all is a seed of selfless thoughts;
Where kindness goes, happiness follows.

Figure 44: THE STREET BEETLE

WHERE IS THE LOVE?

When the streets are filled
By kids of voiceless dreams;
And our homes are full
With gold of endless flow;
Where is the love we claim to share?

When the world is sick
With a ruthless germ;
And our acts are filled
With thoughts of division;
Where is the love we claim to share?

When the voice of war
Roars in our armored base,
And our feet are fast
To born the casualties,
Where is the love we claim to share?

When our smiles are bright
And seem to light the way;
And our hearts are dark
With deeds that spur evil,
Where is the love we claim to share?

When we know the truth
The one which saves the lives;
And we choose to cage
And spread the killing lies;
Where is the love we claim to share?

When we say we love
And form a bond of life;
And tomorrow we're off
To court to share apart;
Where is the love we claim to share?

Our acts are triggered by ego;
Our words beautifully penned;
And our minds with choices to choose
But where is the love when we choose evil?

FOR THE SAKE OF GOLD

There's a time I know
Back from long ago;
When without gold,
Love didn't go;
Engaging with a ring of old
From granny or another soul;
Wasn't there though
But was only told.

The world I know
Is a sea of gold;
For the sake of gold:
Love will overflow,
And secrets will unfold.

For the sake of gold:
The truth they know and hold

Will die silently untold;
The love they fight and mold
Might never grow so old.

Beautiful souls are sold,
To gain the fame and gold;
Smiling death awaits the 'go!'
To fridge their bodies cold.

Beauty from head to toe
Is poised by the smile of gold;
Yet for the sake of gold,
Talent will die unknown.

But this is what I know:
Gold might be sweet like gold,
But gold can not afford a soul;
Gold is a devil's sunny loan.

IMPORTED FOR HER BODY

Beautiful, lovely Lemue
Precious daughter of Africa:
Is the African soil so restless?
Why are you dethroning our green home?

They told you India was a safe-haven,
They said in Lebanon gold is lady-free;
Consigned like goods from home to Qatar,

You thought there life was sweeter and better;
Trading your woman pride with a valueless stranger,
You're trafficked like drugs, from Japan to China;
To Asia, to Europe and else abroad!
Are their pastures truly greener than home's?

Beautiful body and lovely eyes,
Charming voice and sunny smiles,
Money from pleasure is yearning for you;
Forced on arrival to pay your debts
See as you cry in the arms of strangers!

Family home is waiting for you...
Daughter abroad will send good news;
None will comprehend your life so new,
But love is all your assaulted job...

Where is your pride and passport from home?
Locked in a room for business love...
Fed like a pet in a homeless cage,
The men will pay to lose their weights
Is your body a sporting ground?

Traded abroad by your own brother
Your lone dream was to cross the border
And now what is the way further?
Home, sweet home; nowhere like home.

HELLO MONEY

Are you a human crush?
For you they seem to rush!
Imagining the depth of your beauty,
I still think you're so ugly...

Some told me you do speak
But I see no lips nor beak;
On you, the poor will hide and crush
But the rich will have and still rush.

I was told you can save and heal
And I yet was told you hate and kill;
Which side of the coin thus are you;
The bad and ugly or the good?

You cause all men to flirt
For you, they extra miles like birds
Are you a demi super god?
What is this charm you've got?
Gush! I love-hate you, I hate-love you
Do you love humans too?

Money, you engage men and divorce some
Breaking hearts without you,
But if I told you; I love you,
Will you stay with me till death do part?

Figure 45: HELLO MONEY

GUANTANAMO

'Kwarah!' his chains disarmed their frown
And drummed the sleeping ground
Then in every sound,
He heard the voice of freedom
Summoning his convicted name
As he walked towards the door
To quit his angry cell...
Then a sudden stop
At the ajared door
He looked back
With a gloomy smile
At his tiny bed;
It was the softest being
Amongst all he had seen

In that prison scene...

As he walked down the hall way,
Claps and shouts from cells
Innocent and guilty alike
Teens and men I saw;
Each praising freedom
To charm her graceful smile
And catch the wings of their hopes
Not to fly away...
As they cheered him to the door
Each hoping their dawn will smile...

Innocent or guilty he was,
I know not well myself
But I saw a man
With drops of tears within
Walking like a snail,
Eager like to run
To quit those gates of captivity
And feel the warmth of liberty.

As he stepped out of the tyrant gate
Waving goodbye to the crying hands
That one could spot from hanging holes;
He breathed the air of liberty
And whispered to himself:
'...free at last...'
Yet life was never the same
For his fame had drowned to shame.

LET IT GO

People will call you sort of names
Even when dreams have crowned you fame;
For all, you will never be good enough
As long as you account their random thoughts;
Does it matter anyway!
Just let it go!

You may love people like glittering gold
And crave them joy they never know;
They may love you just like bronze
Don't get the light so crude or wrong...
The sun and moon won't shine alike;
Love even more anyway,
Just let it go!

I know the good book reads and says;
Do for others your desired pay...
And then you sow all your smiles
Like moonlight in their nights
Yet their gratitude
Flees your attitude;
Don't stop the good work anyway!
Just let it go.

People will hurt you like wildfire
Till this one life so retires;
And if you're lucky, '...sorry...'
Long as you hold them, you worry;
They're not hooked on you anyway!
Just let it go.

There's more to a smile
Than its diamond light;
Even when your smile grows so old
That your molars just so let you go,
Hold on to life anyway
The breath of life is the seed of hope.

Walk away like scared turtle
Maybe slowly like a wanted snail
Run if you can like a chetah;
But never camouflage like a 'meleon'
To suit the desires of people
All must dwell together anyway
Just let it go.

Figure 46: *LET IT GO*

BARREN WORLD

So much love to give
All in hearts that do not care;
So many smiles to share
All on faces with deep despair
I'm scared of every peeping tomorrow
She seems to nurse nothing but sorrow.

Society is in dying need
Yearning for men who freely give
Giving their most with no strings to meet;
Sometimes it's just a stray smile
That kills a sightless frown;
Sometimes a word from the heart
Revives the greens of the past;
Gold isn't all we do so need.

We needn't work like caterpillars
To fence the future's pride
We've got Just you and I
Like arms of a single being.

Do you too yearn for that tomorrow
Where breaking news will be of peace
Of love and grateful deeds;
To wake from bed every morning
To find no joy in mourning
To sin and truly be sorry
And hope out without worry!

I'm hawking the streets of Haiti

Fellowshipping with hungry stomachs;
I'm smuggling into Afghanistan
To rebuild the walls of war,
I cry for no one sees
That peace is a key to live;
And for the bereaved of nations unseen
Tears like the sea won't bring back beings
Yet let's cry and shade off the pain
If none still sees nor care...

Do we still hope for a 'Superman'
To strangle war and dwell as one?
If all we do is hatching war,
Then we're molding a barren world!
We trade our peace for victory
Be it for fame or gold we need?
No sacrifice is worth a waved-off Peace
No love is worth more than life;
The world is barren without love.

ANGER

The rage of anger brings solitude
Leading to things that steal attitude
Forgetting the things that deem gratitude
But so sad is the tale of its magnitude...

"Anger rests in the bosom of a fool"
Filled with the rage of needless revenge...
To do the things tomorrow might regret.

Anger is the mother of hate;
Born in the clinic of unforgiveness,
She is sensitive like a wild dog
But for the wrong things that need but love.

As poets swap anger to their pens,
Priests pray it out in their tents
While a soldier shoots it out in his gun;
Yet, what happens when anger is gone?

SOLIDARITY

Have you soared across humanity?
Did you see the whereabouts of solidarity?
I saw her hiding in the arms of insincerity
Ashamed because she seems a nonentity
As she murmured about in a soliloquy...
Lurking Like desert wind in her scarcity
That none seems to breathe with liberty

Though she's single and free in simplicity.

As I flew on the wings of curiosity,
I found the smiles of generosity
Just in the hearts of a minority;
Could this be part of the poverty
That wallows in streets of a majority?

I ate from the palms of generosity
Though with little, but for her solidarity,
I saw the heart of true humanity;
Giving their dear as a necessity
And oh! With all sincerity.

To share is a seed of maturity
That saves the face of all humanity;
Whether nonentity or celebrity
All are one in the big Trinity
To dwell in love and eternal unity.

Figure 47: *SOLIDARITY*

A NEW DAY

Night and dreams fading away;
Ushering my being into a new day,
Prime memories of yesterday
Streaming back in reality's sway,
So I gamble my thoughts about;
Thanking the Sky for being allowed
This gift of life; from then till now;
Remembering the plans and all the vows.
Fringing thoughts of doubt and hope,
Battling like soldiers to shape today;
While I wrap my being in the alms nature
Paving my path toward twilight's spy;
Then as I listen to the cheering birds sing,
I rise like the glowing sun ready to win.

THE RACE

Everyone is running
All in the hunt of money
Striking to write a story
To make their tomorrow sunny.
Scrambling for gold to be wealthy
Even the rich are still running ...
Life is sour like lemons; sweet like honey
And when time is truly come to glory ,
A flock of birds will announce the trophy
But all it needs is a goal so worthy.

GONE

Smiles are never gone
We just ignore in storms;
Smiles are like the sun:
Like day it comes
Like night it's gone.

Life is not a marathon
Doesn't matter who won!
Men of integrity never run
Just live the life like fun;
For even in victory all will be gone.

Yes, we'll all be gone
Swept in a thousand years to come
And the tears of the sky will mourn
But must men leave by the gun?
We compose our own death songs.

Men rise like cocks at dawn
Their peaceful mares forgone
Possessed with dreams unborn;
They hawk the streets and worn
Through age and soon are gone.

Unknown we soon are born
We grow from weak to strong
Smile like sun at dawn
To look back and say we won
And someday like sun are gone
Gone to never come.

HAPPY TEARS

A stream of torrential tears down his cheeks
That broke the stems of his hairy smile;
They ran down like a waterfall
Along in the warm arms of gravity
To feed the hungry, yearning soil.

Evoking his sleeping emotions,
His lips rolled away like a Jesus tomb
Then a set of happy molars shone
Dividing themselves into glorious laughter;
And the breaking news from his tone
Was the loviest song I've ever heard;
It sounded like a morning bird song
Awaking happiness from her hiding place.

I wouldn't forget the spirit of love
That I saw dancing within him;
Now he needed the mightiest hug
From the one nearest his beating heart;
As his tears rolled down in their silent flee
Eroding his fears to bring forth glee.

Happiness will make you cry
Just like the clouds in the mighty sky;
Big or small you so maybe
That feeling of joy will jump in you
Shading your hurt like dry leaves of a tree;
All we want is to live and be happy
It's the greatest feeling we can ever carry.

Figure 48: HAPPY TEARS

HAPPINESS IS GORGEOUS

I caught the cutest smile I've ever seen;
I'm still wondering if it's from an earthly being;
Her joy erupted like magma from deep within,
Even the birds are still so amazed!

To love is such a good thing,
But to love and be loved is to be happy;
Spreading your smile like a baby without worry
To scare sorrow from the path to honor.
Everyone yearns to be happy,
Even the one known as enemy;
Doing the things you normally wouldn't
To wear the smile you normally couldn't.

Happiness is not the glittering gold
But the true smiles you wouldn't let go;
It comes like fever from deep within
To portray a smile you cannot explain;
It leaps like a baby in a woman's womb
To announce the advent of a beautiful thing.

Happiness may leave without reason
Draining your smiles into a lonely prison;
But she'll come back without apology;
For the freedom of a thousand smiles,
For the mending of broken hearts,
And for the dethroning of tyrant sorrow;

Figure 49*:* **HAPPINESS IS GORGEOUS**

MOTHER EARTH & NATURE POEMS

This section embodies a cross-section of poems that appreciate the beauty of nature. The poems in gross are written in favor of nature protection and preservation.

MOTHER EARTH
(Appreciating Nature)

You shield us up like a fetus in the womb
Under your sky and your sun like a room;
We feed on you like a host with our food
Consuming your beauty like a fire in the bush;
Maybe we're greedy; maybe we're rude
Yet like a mother you're ages good
To harbor our breath and give us your moon.

You give us the moon to see our way
Enchanting our hope with the gift of your day;
You give us the air; we breathe without pay
Like a mother, never aborting our stay.

You cry for your rain to wash our tears
When we go wrong, you thunder in fear;
Iterating your love with the beautiful rainbow
And protecting us from the aliens' bow.

Give to the earth all your meaning
The beauty in you; you've been dreaming;
Show it you aren't just existing;

But breathing, living and exhibiting.
We take the trees and the breeze
Breathing its air; fresh and free;
What is it worth a living;
If we're living like stingy without giving?

For the roots of earth are dying
And no tears seem to be crying;
Even when we die and are weeping,
She folds us up eternally sleeping...
A motherly love I have never seen.

Figure 50: MOTHER EARTH

PLIGHT OF THE MOON

My name is Miss Moon
I'm single and searching for a groom;
Though I walk about so bright,
Humble and beautiful like a bride;
I'm still lonely amongst a thousand stars.

I cross the sky like a prostitute at night;
Falling in love with stars only by sight,
They smile at me as I motion so bright;
But it seems I'm just a slay queen in the sky
I'm still lonely amongst a thousand stars.

When I come across a sinister of clouds,
Knowing my beauty will not be allowed;
Humbly, I keep my bright pride so low
As I motion across in a scary flow;
I'm still lonely amongst a thousand stars.

I'm a lady of my own pride
Measuring myself to non but mine;
The sun might light all through the day,
But I'll rule the sky when time comes my way;
I will always be the queen moon...
Ruling the night without a king groom.

HELLO WINTER

It's yet a beautiful day in the county
As summer frowns at the sight of winter;
Smiling trees with green feelings
As birds flee from the shadows of cold;
All scrambling for the sympathy of the sun.

Wooly blanket in bed with Quinta
Scared of the smile of happy winter;
Ocean in ice to dare the swimmer
Scared of the beach in the heart of winter;
Charcoal in hell; dry wood will suffer
To burn the cold of the angry winter;
While family unite by the chimney fire
Patient for the season of winter retired.

The ships go angry
As the wind plays crazy;
The dress is sweeter
As the cold is bitter;
And the heart cold-shivers
To pull a love trigger.

THE NIGHTTIME SAGA

To sleep the sun is gone;
And the night still young!
The moon yawning
While the stars are rising
Like babies in the morning.

Dream land travelers
Lodging their last supper
Into their vacant bellies
For the long night journey;
While warm bed sheets
Yearn for tired weight
To take-off to dreamland.

It's yet the heart of the night
Earth haunted by forms unseen;
Could they be living beings?
I know not well myself...
Bats and badgers go so free
Owls and Blackhawks in the trees
As the silent night knows no peace.

Cats like bats scaring the night
As nightmares flee
To meet the gone dawn;
Again the sun will yawn
To sleep the moon is gone;
It's yet a new dawn.

WAR & SACRIFICE

There's a lot in war just more than the fighting; the sacrifice of what is most precious: the lives of men and women and children. Society is still doomed with war here and there, in spite of modernity. War may be of greed, but its wounds are beyond repairs. War and sacrifice are the main themes that run through this section.

HOMELESS HOME
(In solidarity with all refugees)

The tale is that of wars;
The wars that broke their walls,
Once upon a time was peace
Then came a time they lived without ease;
Brother against brother, soldier against civilians
Driven by ego and ego of politicians.

They're not foot soldiers
Yet in pain they trek Across the fields;
They're not sea divers
Yet they swim across the wild waters;
Miles to cover; day and night; foot to foot
Women like children matching about without food

Loaded with weights like donkeys,
They hide in trees like monkeys;
In hunt of a place with peace as a key;

It's the politics men play
That leave others astray.

In search of love
In search of shelter
In search of pasture
In search of peace...
Away from home.

Where else should there be peace if not home?
See their tears because they're not aborigines;
See the bodies vomited by the sea ashore;
See their dry skins as they cross the deserts
Just like the scales on basking lizards.

Gratitude to the hearts that care;
That make life for them so fair,
We do not love if we hate strangers;
They come in peace and not like rangers.

I may not have penned enough
To vomit their swallowed plights,
But wherever you find them,
Hug them with true love...
Let the tears that rain their hearts not be in vain.

Figure 51: **HOMELESS HOME**

SACRIFICE

Sacrifice is a frightful price of war;
Duty keeps calling... saying;
'...Defend the nation from falling...'
Soldier man sacrificing
His life; and family crying;
So, there comes a day... 'knock, knock',
And he is gone without a '...bye...'

Sacrifice is a shameless price of love;
Knocking at the gate of the heart...
Filled with hurt and blinded deeds;

To mend beautiful souls for life.

Sacrifice is an enduring price of freedom;
Hunted by men of selfless wisdom;
To assemble love in dreaded kingdoms,
So, Mandela and Luther sang to freedom.

Sacrifice is a gift of choice;
Born in fear-possessing hope;
Walking in men with voiceless voices,
Just like the thunder that carries the rains
Down to earth from gloomy clouds.

Figure 52: SACRIFICE

PEACE

Peace should be the sun
That shines in all season;
But peace is like an oasis
We search with all reason.

Peace should be a song
We sing like one citizen;
But peace is like a church bell
We ring from time to time.

Peace should be the old age
We can't restrict from coming;
But peace is like the beauty
It has the power to fade away.

Peace should be the sky
We see each day and night;
But peace is like the clouds
That come and vapor away.

Peace should be the water;
Irreplaceable in nature;
But peace is like the liquor
We really can do without...

Peace should be for all
Not just for some with power;
Peace should be a natural law
Not just a law with conditions;

But peace is now a weapon
Left in the cold hands of death;
And bargained by men with debts;
Peace cries for redemption and propagation.

MEET THE HEROES

We'll travel the world free of this virus;
Sailing like a fish from Europe through Cyprus
To meet the heroes that came from zero.

We'll run from Jamaica to Kingston
Dancing to the reggae of Bob Marley;
But we wouldn't smoke his wheat back to Mali.

We'll fly from America to Washington
Paying our great honor to Martin Luther;
But we wouldn't smuggle racism out of borders.

We'll move from South Africa to Pretoria
Hailing in Zulu the love of Mandela;
But we'll burn the traces of apartheid like Adolf Hitler.

We'll stream from Nigeria to Abuja
Visiting the streets of Nnamdi Azikiwe;
Igbo or Yoruba, we wouldn't be virused by tribalism.

Visa free from Asia to Afghanistan and then India
To assimilate the wisdom of Theresa and Gandhi;
But we'll evoke the spirit of Bin Ladden
To tell him terrorism is not a problem solution.

We'll trek across Africa like camels;
Honoring the courage of: Lumumba and Nkrumah;
The steadfastness of Kagame, Annan and Kenyatta;
To send a message of victory back to the world;
But we wouldn't be infected by African low self esteem.

We'll pop and brake from Ethiopia to Addis Ababa
Chanting 'They don't care' of Micheal Jackson;
But we wouldn't bleach our color for any reason.

Sailing like a fish from Greece to Athens
To savor the antiques of Alexander the Great;
Reminding France colonialism is of ancient times.

We'll corrupt our way from Cameroon to Yaoundé
Craving to meet the legendary Roger Miller;
But we wouldn't be infected by forever leadership.

We'll soar like an eagle from England to London
Starving to peep the beauty of Queen Elizabeth;
But we wouldn't isolate ourselves as Brexit.

We'll sneak like ants from China to Beijing
And even if we can't play in the movies with Jet Li,
We'll warn them to stop testing things
That endanger world security.

If we could fly like angels,
We'll abdicate the beauty of heaven
To take their righteous deeds back to life
Divorcing the world of this ruthless virus;
We starve for heroes like never before.

IF SOMEONE WILL LISTEN

For so long we've heard nothing
But dooms of guns that keep knocking;
Chained by fear in our homes
But even home is not safe for hope;
We've pledged our tears to the world
To name an end to this war,
The soil has drunk our blood
But our wounds are yet to clot...

How long will we keep fighting?
Till that end, will we still be breathing?
Though we cry, no one seems to see
Like a sinking ship in the deep of the sea;
We've known what it feels like to be home
Now stranded in the world like alone...
As we linger from place to place
Like early men without a trace.

Our pride is stolen
Our homes are broken;
Great souls have fallen
Lost hopes forgotten.

To the memory of the lost and rotten
Irreplaceable lives our soil begotten
Buried by nature and forgotten;
They die in vain if tomorrow can't smile
As we hope for the sight of a tunnel light

We seem lost in a world of thinking men
With our knees on the floor still bent;
If our dreams still linger in fears
And fellow men can't see our crying tears
Does anyone truly care?

CASUALTIES

I have been to the battle fields
And I have seen the golden seals
Of soldiers on their open graves
As their loved ones wail and crave...
They did nothing to loose them
If only tears could undo the dead!

I walked across the silent city
I found a child drowned in pity
Her tears drizzling upon a corpse
Gone is her only living dream;
What hope is there left in her little being?

I caught a bullet of misery
Straying across the broken city;
Then a woman and child I saw
They were simply the fallouts of war
Defenseless, 'gunless' and lifeless;
If the bullets be so fearless,
Why are hearts this careless?

Then I looked upon in the noisy clouds;
Shadows of crying souls in a crowd
Maybe their time wasn't right,
Maybe they still want to fight
Can they buy back the hand of time?
See who's here that pays the price;
A little baby without left or right.

Pregnant women here and there

Stray bullets that do not care;
Gone like a soldier who never fought
Even when its life was still a thought;
And then the future in bleeding tears
When it knows posterity will not appear.

They're all casualties without their will
All they loved; the bullet did steal;
Helpless like orphans without meal
Those who kill, do they ever feel?

Figure 53: **CASUALTIES**

TOGETHER AS ONE

Of the days we cry
Are the times we smile
When we cry together
Consoling each other
Like sister and brother
From different mothers.

As the sorrows come
And our smiles are gone;
Together we must stand
Hand in hand;
Divided we shall fall
And our victory is won.

Though we fight the other,
We fight our own brothers;
They're just stool leaders
With the law and order.

So we do not fight to steal
Neither a bird do we have to kill;
But for what is just and also right
For tomorrow to be bright;
But as we rise,
Remember the price;
Hovering alive together
Like sisters and brothers.

FOR THE FALLEN

A moment of silence for the fallen!
...
At the summit of the fallen battle
Where smiles have lost their lights
As the soil drinks oozing blood
Drizzling from the lips of green wounds;
Tired borders carried the weights
Of helpless soldiers; dead and weak.

While the vultures celebrate in the sky
The victory of battle they never fought
As butties of copses lie below
Under the trees and plain of battle;
Craving for graves they never may find.

Even the courage of their guns
Couldn't stop their quitting souls
Their bleeding bodies eroded
When the fierce bullet came knocking.

Some died like virgins without a spring
To uphold their names now they're gone;
Some died in silence like sunset
Who bears the darkness their absence brings?
But all they died like martyrs
Denying themselves to honor the nation.

Nations may weep, weep, weep...
For their fallen soldiers in a week
But family will bleed, bleed, bleed...

Tears in sorrow so hard to quit...

And for the one thing I saw;
They fought not to win
Nor did they to loose;
Even if winning was their desire,
They fought to die
If that it costs to serve the nation;
...
A moment of silence for the fallen.

Figure 54: FOR THE FALLEN

DESPAIR & HOPE

Poems in this section are typically mixed; and the theme runs though despair and hope. The poems capture empathy, sadness, self esteem and a lot more to boost the human from within.

YOU'RE BEAUTIFUL

Don't mind the pain that steals your smile
It's only jealous because of you;
You're the most beautiful creature it's ever seen.

Don't mind the sorrow that peeps like hate
It's only amazed because of you;
You're the most beautiful creature it's ever seen.

Even the Creator marvels at your beauty
Dethroning heaven to feel His creation;
You're the most beautiful creature Heaven made.

See the birds, do they cry?
Aren't they creatures like you and I?
Men will rush for gold not stones
Pain will come for you not birds
You're the most beautiful creature nature knows.

You're beautiful.

Figure 55: **YOU'RE BEAUTIFUL**

HOPE WILL NEVER LEAVE

She stood in front of the mirror
Dressed in black like a widow;
She called herself a failure
For gone are the things she treasured;
Then she watched her running tears
As they fled away in fears;
With her sad heart full of violence,
She sobbed in dead silence.

But then she realized:
She was being self-criticized,
She's got the strength and beauty,
To start all over and not be guilty,
'Why am I standing here mourning?'
As she left for work that morning...
Hope will never leave
Sometimes we just let it be.

AFTERWARD

One day I surely will be gone;
Gone from this play ground alone
To a place only my earthly life will tell;
Some may cry and some may laugh;
Some may think I will be back;
But in all, it will be the end.

When I'm gone in that beautiful spring
Or in that sunny summer as time please,
Cry the tears as much as you can
If only they'll form a river to newer birth;
But I tell you what, each drop will be in vain.

Cry and tell the world I was a good being;
Tell them I fought such a good fight
Just like a saint in my earthly life;
Tell them I dreamt to make the world a better place;

But it will be in vain if I fought alone;
Hint them in all I might be in heaven.

But also cry and tell them of my lies;
Tell them of that truth I hit in my files;
Tell them of the love I showed not to all;
And of those times I forsook the gospel call;
If we both did, tell them you were there;
Hint them in all I might have reached hell.

I will not in your dreams to tell where I am;
Heaven or hell then, the choice wouldn't be mine;
Hell is for real and Heaven is free;
The price is paid for you and me...
But earth is a place to make the choice.

WITHOUT A FRIEND

A quest of friends on Facebook
All you've got is a picture to look;
A friendly stranger,
A talk on messenger;
A host of friends you'll never meet;
You're still lonely without a friend.

You club the streets with a swam of friends
Company and party are sweet like honey
Then they back-stink you like angry bees,
Home alone like a cloudy moon

You're still lonely without a friend.

You had faith in love like a believer
You thought you found your love redeemer
The love is withdrawn; not even a friend;
You're still lonely without a friend.

Can you walk in a friendless journey?
It reduces some friendship troubles!
Company is never always permanent
Even your shadow quits when the sun is gone,
And you're still lonely without a friend.

If you should hate a friend for a fault,
Play a hate song from a hate tape
So the words may soon fade away;
But none is flawless that be your friend
Play them a love song from deep in your heart
Even when you're lonely apart for awhile...
For true words from the heart never fade away;
Times will still come when you're lonely without a friend.

SOMEBODY

Everybody need somebody
To scare some sorrow and buy some company;
Just love somebody
Should it mean to borrow your love to that buddy;
Just care for somebody
Forgetting the fame of your tearful story;
Just love somebody, friend, stranger, family.

Somebody needs your voice and smile
That smile you do so hide,
To dry their tears and light their day;
Unfrown that face with a gorgeous smile!
Whenever you worry of the things you're sorry,
And your burden is so heavy to carry;
Take a walk and voice to somebody
For tomorrow you might find nobody.

I know somebody that knows somebody
I love somebody like else nobody;
Without somebody, life is a lonely beauty;
Friend, family and stranger...
But somebody needs somebody:
To make some money in the mask of company.

We all do need somebody,
Nobody is a nobody;
Without somebody,
The world is lonely
Like Mercury..
Respect for everybody.

ORPHAN OF HOPE

She cried so loud but all in silence
Her thoughts fighting like a mob in violence;
And though her pain was deep and loud,
No one seemed to see nor hear...
For all her tears did flow within in fear.

'I'm a daughter of hope...' she said
Consoling her heart and soul within;
She thought life could only offer a frown
But like Everest, she stood her sandy ground
Still hoping to wear the victory crown.

Then came a time her hope was dead
She emptied a space by the side of her heart
Throwing away some beauty reserves
To mutilate the corpse of her lost hope;
Wishing that one day, her hope will resurrect
To take away her desert of frowns.

But she was now only an orphan of hope
Harboring a peril she couldn't share,
And crying in silence in her world alone
Yet in all, her 'hope will resurrect' she said
Worshiping its corpse by the side of her heart
Day and night into every tomorrow...
And fighting life's battles with each breath
As she swallowed her sorrow with a smile she borrowed.

BROKEN

Streams of happiness lurking away
Joy asleep and pain awoken
Violent within in screams of silence;
Hope on run, the dreams are sentenced
The mind within in scornful silence.

A bleeding heart and a contrite soul
Broken within like an amoebic bone
As sadness arise, the smiles are garbaged
Dwelling each day in a den of fears;
But time shall heal a broken soul.

A DAY IN PARADISE

Perhaps in my dreams
Perhaps reality knows
Perhaps I was drunk
But this I know I saw;
A day in paradise
A place I'll rather be,
There be a lot to see
Beauty eyes've never met.

I woke like the sunrise
To meet unfading lights:
Roses that never die
Purple, red and white
Aligned the silent shores

Of the shy blue slow river.

Fishes in waters, live!
Swimming across and by,
Fresh trees so ever green
With fruits that never quit;
Four legged; domestic-wild
Dwelling along like one,
And O the birds on choir trees
Music along all day free.

This feeling I wouldn't forget
Happiness never left...;
Sorrow across the gates
Watching with jealous eyes,
And it felt like forever...
A day in paradise
While I'm still alive
There life never dies.

A day in paradise
A place I'll rather be
Where sorrow will never kiss
This joy I've found in me.

MY GREATEST VICTORY

At the foot of the Everest
Where dreams begin as tender guests,
I set out to find my best
To climb my way to the mountain crest;
And within, courage and fear battled
Like eager ships and angry waves.

Haunted by fear and despair,
My walk has been a ceaseless flow
Mounting higher and never below;
The storms still blow
And sometimes I have fallen steps low
To rest like a lake but be on my go;
Mounting steps to a place I know,
Racing against my utmost best
To build a home on that mountain crest.

I keep rising like a shooting seed
Guiding my steps not to wither back deep;
Streams to rivers, rivers to sea,
My greatest victory: my ceaseless walk;
And when I reach that tired crest,
Only then will my feet so rest.

Every End signs a New Beginning.

Milton Keynes UK
Ingram Content Group UK Ltd.
UKHW022200141023
430632UK00020B/745